MARGRET & H.A. REY'S

Curious George

and the Hot Air Balloon

Illustrated in the style of H. A. Rey by Vipah Interactive

Houghton Mifflin Company   Boston

Copyright © 1998 by Houghton Mifflin Company

Based on the character of Curious George®, created by Margret and H. A. Rey.
Illustrated by Vipah Interactive, Wellesley, Massachusetts: C. Becker, D. Fakkel, M. Jensen,
S. SanGiacomo, C. Witte, C. Yu.

The text of this book is set in 17-pt. Adobe Garamond.
The illustrations are watercolor and charcoal pencil, reproduced in full color.

Library of Congress Cataloging-in-Publication Data

Curious George and the hot air balloon / based on the original character by Margret
and H. A. Rey.
p. cm.
Summary: While visiting Mt. Rushmore, Curious George gets into mischief when he takes
an unplanned ride on a hot air balloon.
RNF ISBN 0-395-91918-5 PAP ISBN 0-395-91909-6 PABRD ISBN 0-395-92338-7
[1. Monkeys — Fiction. 2. Hot air balloons — Fiction. 3. Mt. Rushmore National Memorial
(S.D.) — Fiction] I. Rey, Margret, 1906–1996. II. Rey, H. A. (Hans Augusto), 1898–1977.
III. Vipah Interactive
PZ7.C92115 1998
[Fic] — dc21   98-21326
                                                       CIP AC

Manufactured in the United States of America
WOZ 10 9 8 7 6 5 4

This is George.

George was a good little monkey and always very curious.

He was on a trip with his friend, the man with the yellow hat. It was the end of their vacation, and they wanted to make just two more stops.

They were in South Dakota so, of course, they went to see Mount
Rushmore. George had never seen anything like it. "These are the

faces of four great presidents," a tour guide said. "George Washington, Thomas Jefferson, Theodore Roosevelt, and Abraham Lincoln."

"Look!" said a girl.
"There's something crawling
on George Washington's head."
The tour guide explained that some
workers were making repairs to the faces.
George watched the workers.

Then he saw a helicopter fly by. It was taking tourists for a close-up look. George thought that would be fun.

"Maybe we can take a ride later," the man said. "But now we need to leave or we'll be late for the hot air balloon race."

So they got back into their little blue car and before long they came

to a whole field full of hot air balloons. George was delighted to see such big balloons. He liked their spots and stripes and stars, but his favorite had a picture of a bunny on it.

One balloon was not yet up in the air. Its owner was hurrying to fill it as a newspaper reporter took pictures.

The man with the yellow hat watched the balloon on the ground, but George watched the balloons in the sky.

He was curious: why didn't they fly away?
Then he saw the ropes.

A rope is a good thing to keep a balloon
from flying away, thought George. A rope is a
good thing to climb. . . .

Sometimes when a monkey sees something to climb, he can't help himself. He has to climb it.

George thought he would climb just one rope then quickly climb down.

But when George climbed
up, there was no way to climb
back down. The rope had come
undone — and there was only
one place to go.

UP

UP

UP

went the balloon.
And George went
with it.

George flew higher and higher, and the people below grew smaller and smaller.

The man with the yellow hat was tiny. The newspaper reporter was, too. And the owner of the balloon wasn't very big...

but he was big enough for George to see that he was angry!

George felt bad. He didn't mean to take the balloon—he didn't even know how to fly it. As the wind whisked him away, he wished he had someone to help him.

But he was all alone.

George climbed into the basket. When he looked around, he found
he wasn't alone after all. The race was on—and he was in the lead!

Together the balloons flew across the field and over the forest.
Now George was having fun. But before he knew it...

George was alone again, and all the fun was gone.

Flying by himself high in the sky, George was frightened. How would he ever get down? he wondered. Oh, if only he hadn't climbed that rope. . . .

Suddenly the wind changed, and
George saw something familiar.
He was excited—someone was
sure to help him now. In fact, there
was someone right in front of him!

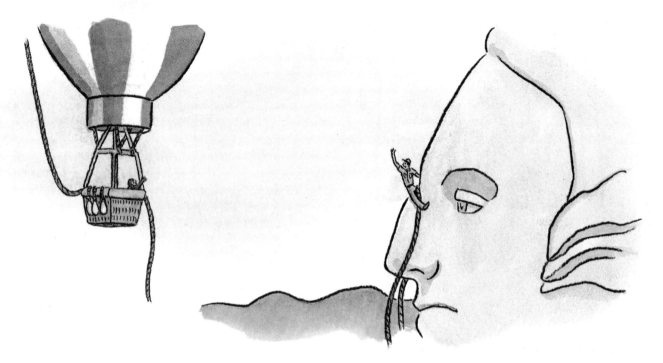

It was one of the workers—and he was stranded on George Washington's nose! George was so happy to see the worker he didn't notice how happy the worker was to see him.

Slowly, the balloon floated closer.

Would it come close enough? It did! The worker grabbed onto the rope and climbed up. Soon he was in the basket with George.

Hurrah, George was rescued!

Hurrah, the worker was rescued, too!

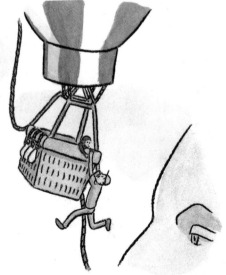

They sailed up over George Washington's head and landed safely in a tree. Soon a whole crowd came to rescue them both.

The man with the yellow hat was happy to see George. The reporter was glad to have such an exciting story to report. And the owner of the balloon wasn't angry anymore.

Everyone had seen the rescue—George was a hero!

After the workers thanked him, George got a special treat—he got to ride in the helicopter.

The helicopter flew George and the man with the yellow hat once more past the presidents, then back to the little blue car.

As they drove away, the man said, "That was some vacation, George!" George agreed. It was an exciting vacation. But they were both very glad to go home.